CHIC
SIMPLE

Components

2.00
2-10-21

"Rubber Duckie, you're the one!

You make bath time lots of fun."

f r o m "Rubber Duckie"

CHIC
SIMPLE
Components

B A T H

ALFRED A. KNOPF NEW YORK 1993

THIS IS A BORZOI BOOK
PUBLISHED BY ALFRED A. KNOPF, INC.

KIM JOHNSON GROSS JEFF STONE
WRITTEN BY JUDITH NEWMAN
PHOTOGRAPHS BY MARIA ROBLEDO
ICON ILLUSTRATION BY ERIC HANSEN
RESEARCHED BY KIMBERLY PASQUALE
STYLED BY ANITA CALERO

DESIGN AND ART DIRECTION BY ROBERT VALENTINE
INCORPORATED

Grateful acknowledgment is made to Festival Attractions, Inc., for permission
to reprint an excerpt from "Rubber Duckie," words and music by Jeff Moss,
copyright © 1970 by Festival Attractions, Inc. Reprinted by permission.

Library of Congress Cataloging-in-Publication Data
Gross, Kim Johnson.
Chic simple: bath/Kim Johnson Gross, Jeff Stone, and Judith Newman.
p. cm. – (Chic simple)
ISBN 0-679-42763-5
1. Bathing customs. 2. Bathing accessories. I. Stone, Jeff. II. Newman, Judith.
III. Title. IV. Title: Bath. V. Series.
GT2845.G76 1993
391'.64–dc20
93-20310
CIP

Manufactured in the United States of America
First Edition

CONTENTS

"The more you know, the less you need."

Chic Simple is a primer for living well but sensibly in the 1990s. It's for those who believe that quality of life does not come in accumulating things, but in paring down to the essentials, with a commitment to home, community, and the environment. In a world of limited resources, Chic Simple enables readers to bring value and style into their lives with economy and simplicity.

T H E   B A T H

BATH. 1: The action of bathing or immersing the body, or a part of it. 2: A receptacle, apartment, or place for bathing. —*The Oxford English Dictionary*
BATH. A kind of mystic ceremony substituted for religious worship, with what spiritual efficacy has not been determined. —Ambrose Bierce, *The Devil's Dictionary*

"I am in love with moistness."
GEORGE ELIOT, *The Mill on the Floss*

THE HISTORY OF THE BATH.

IN THE BEGINNING THERE WAS WATER, SUN, AND TIME. THE BATH WAS A HOT SPRING OR ROILING brook; man traveled to water before the water could travel to him. With the advent of the aqueduct, suddenly water flowed where we wished: the Roman baths were a communal meeting ground where men could gather. It wasn't until the eighteenth century that the bath became a private sanctuary. The first formal bathtub arrived in America in the early 1800s, when Benjamin Franklin imported the French sabotière. Made of copper and shaped like a shoe, it had a furnace in the "heel" to heat water.

"If you go long enough without a bat

TAKING A BATH IN 1901

The first person to go over Niagara Falls in a barrel was a woman, Anna Edson Taylor, on October 24, 1901.

TAKING A BATH IN THE 1980s

Ivan Boesky, Michael Milken, Donald Trump, Leona Helmsley

BLOOD BATHS

1. *Jean-Paul Marat, assassinated in his tub by Charlotte Corday*
2. *The three wives of George Smith—all drowned. His bathtub is now installed in Madame Tussaud's Wax Museum* 3. *Dorothy Sayers's novel,* Whose Body: *"The stark naked body was lying in the tub."*
4. *Michael Caine's patients in* Dressed to Kill
5. *Glenn Close in* Fatal Attraction

ROMANTIC BATHS

1. *Doris Day and Rock Hudson in* Pillow Talk
2. *Robin Williams and Maria Conchita Alonso in* Moscow on the Hudson 3. *Marisa Berenson and Ryan O'Neal in* Barry Lyndon
4. *William Hurt and Kathleen Turner in* Body Heat

en the fleas will let you alone." ERNIE PYLE

Cleanse. "Home in Three Days. Don't Wash." That was Napoleon's message to his wife, Josephine; his preference for women au naturel was not unusual for the times. The popularity of bathing has ebbed and flowed: the Romans and Egyptians were obsessed with personal hygiene, but with the rise of Christianity and the association of bathing with sensuality and self-indulgence, grime prevailed. Saint Francis of Assisi considered an unwashed body a badge of piety; Queen Isabella of Castile boasted that she had had only two baths in her life—at birth and right before her marriage. Puritans considered bathing impure, and laws in Pennsylvania and Virginia either banned or limited the activity. In the 1890s, women in America were enjoined not to bathe more than once a week, as it was thought that the water would sap them of feminine energies. Today, we link bodily cleanliness with honesty and dependability. "He's clean," we say, in the vernacular—and we know we're safe.

Relaxation. A creak of spigots, a whoosh of hot water, the drip of the tap, and silence: in the bath we create our own private watery world. The ancient Greek word "to bathe" also meant "to drive sadness from the mind": a soak makes today's problems trivial and tomorrow's problems solvable. According to a recent study, 46% of women relax by taking a bath, as compared with 20% of men. More men would indulge if they knew what architects know: men sound better singing in the bath than women, because the tiles are made of materials that resonate to lower frequencies.

BEST BATHTUB MUSIC

Wagner's "Liebestod"

James Brown's "Hot Pants"

Handel's "Water Music"

Ella Fitzgerald singing Cole Porter

Anything by Mel Tormé

Bobby Darin singing "Splish Splash"

BATHTUB READING

Raymond Chandler's The Long Goodbye

Jane Austen's Pride and Prejudice

Bram Stoker's Dracula

Stack of trashy magazines

WARNING: DON'T GET TOO RELAXED

Every day, one American drowns in the bathtub.

Medicinal. In *The Sting*, Paul Newman eased his hangover in a tub full of ice cubes, but the bath needn't be the aqueous equivalent of cod-liver oil to cure what ails you. For centuries, bathing has been used to relieve a variety of ills, from eczema to rheumatoid arthritis. Men, are you having fertility problems? Take a few cold baths a week. Sperm needs to be several degrees below body temperature to survive; it's friskier in cool environs. At times, baths were even used to cure madness. "There, go to Bath with you!"(which meant "Don't talk nonsense!") was a common expression in nineteenth-century England, when insane people were sent to the town of Bath to regain their senses in the healing mineral waters there.

GINGER *Gingerroot, boiled in hot water and massaged into the scalp, can get rid of dandruff.* EPSOM SALTS *A handful of Epsom salts relieves constipation.* OATMEAL *A few cups of oatmeal in the bath soothes itchy skin.* EUCALYPTUS *When inhaled, unclogs sinuses.*

Sensual. To lie in a pool of hot water, slicked by oil or tickled by the suds, is to rediscover the child inside oneself. Hair swirling underwater is a sea creature; a breast breaks through and the water lapping against it is a wave against a boulder. A whiff of tea rose; bebop of hot and cold as steam evaporates off the skin's surface; and the embrace of thick-piled towels redolent of Ivory soap. Reveling in the pleasures of the body, we become disembodied. Do those ten toes way down there really belong to me? However much our bodies may annoy us, underwater we appreciate them anew. Everyone is beautiful in the bathtub.

SEX
Bathing together is the most popular sexual activity besides sex: according to one census, more than forty-three million couples have taken baths together.

SEXY
*Percentage of females who like the way they look naked: 22%
Percentage of males: 68%*

SEX—NOT
In fifteenth-century Arabia, those who used communal baths were exempt from taxes.

Invigorating. Some use the bath to drop out; for others, it's the place to tune in. We have brainstorms; we do deals; we whisper conspiratorially to our lovers on phones, planning what the night will bring. Winston Churchill dictated to his secretary from the bath; he also practiced his speeches there. He once postponed an important speech to the Council of Europe because the hot water in his home had run out. Perhaps when we're submerged, trace memories of the womb allow us to tap into some primitive creative force (or perhaps water just feels good). Edmond Rostand reportedly penned *Cyrano de Bergerac* in the tub.

ENERGIZING BATH
RECIPE

Pour into a bath any one of several essential oils that give the skin and the brain a buzz: ginseng, peppermint, and eucalyptus are favorites.

INVIGORATING
BATH

An invigorating bath needn't be cold—but ending with a cold splash can be a restorative, particularly in cold weather. It helps retain body heat.

SCHEMING BATH

Joan Crawford, afloat in bubbles and rage, plotted her friend's downfall in George Cukor's The Women, *1939*

Fragrant. Smell influences our moods in ways we barely recognize; we form first impressions with our eyes, but lingering impressions with our noses. In the bath, fragrance encircles us like the arms of a lover. Stimulants such as lemon and peppermint allow us to face the day; relaxants such as chamomile and lavender let us wind down in the evening. More and more bath products today are scented with hundreds of natural flowers, fruits, and vegetables: casaba melon and sunflowers, linden and orange blossom, juniper and pine—a medley of odors that can make us remember or help us forget.

AROMATHERAPY AT A GLANCE

Invigorating Scents
clove, rosemary, spruce, juniper, lemon, peppermint

Stress Relievers
vanilla, nutmeg, orange

Relaxants
jasmine, chamomile, marjoram, lavender, rose

Aphrodisiacs
sandalwood, ylang-ylang, sage

Simple Bath. Water. A vessel. Flesh. That's all that's really needed for the simple bath. It's a secular baptism, a call to the faithful for restoring body, mind, and spirit. Medieval monks bathed in cold water as a penance; Gloria Swanson soaked only in bottled waters. The human animal sheds its skin about 899 times during its lifetime. In the bath, we are renewed; by sloughing off dead skin, we literally allow our inner selves to surface.

"From the roof he saw a woman washing herself; and the woman was very beautiful."

2 SAM. 11:2,
David espying Bathsheba

BASIC TEMPERATURE
Between ninety and ninety-five degrees. Anyone with pulmonary problems should avoid higher temperatures, because hot water dilates the blood vessels and forces the heart to pump faster.

BASIC TIME
No longer than fifteen minutes, no more than twice a day. Any more than this could irritate the skin.

BASIC PHYSICS
Archimedes' Principle
An immersed object is buoyed up by a force equal to the fluid it displaces.

4 Basic Elements. Bath products have become the tail that wags the dog: with Americans spending $700 million a year on bath products, they are now the largest segment of the cosmetics industry. Surprising, really, when you consider that all you need for the bath is WATER, soap, a scrubber for removing dirt and dead skin, and a towel for drying. The raging debate between shower and bath enthusiasts: which gets the body cleaner? SOAP industry experts seem to agree: the bath. In order to get really clean, we must remove dirt, oil, and flakes of dead skin. But a SCRUB alone won't do it. The skin must be hydrated, which takes lots of soaking. The average American spends about eleven minutes in the shower and twenty minutes in the bath. There's one caveat about bath use: since soap floats on top of the bathwater, there's a thin film left on the body when you stand up. So a total cleaning means a quick shower and a TOWEL-off after a dip.

"Soap and education are
not as sudden as a massacre,
but they are more deadly in
the long run."

MARK TWAIN

E L E M E N T S

What was once a trip to the laboratory is now a trip to the jungle: that's the difference between yesterday's bath ingredients and today's. The Nineties bath is about purity: what goes into the bath ingredients must eventually find its way back to the environment without damaging our water supplies, our skin, or our fellow creatures.

"When you take a bath, you are civilized; when you don't take a bath, you are cultured."

LIN YUTANG

Skin Types. One mile of blood vessels, five miles of nerves: our skin is our cocoon, the protective layering between ourselves and the world. It breathes for us, shields us from roving ultraviolet rays and microbes; it allows us the sense of touch, our most primitive source of pleasure. We take what the skin does for granted; instead, we worry, How does it look? We all seek the honeyed glow of Nabokov's nymphet; with the help of bath oils, salts, powders, and bubbles, we settle for the best our genes can give us.

FOR DRY OR AGING SKIN: *Look for products heavy on the humectants (ingredients that seal moisture into skin) such as mineral oil, chamomile oil, and aloe vera, the cactuslike plant long known for its ability to soothe burns.* **FOR OILY SKIN:** *Avoid "fatted" soaps—opt for soaps with oatmeal, or natural astringents like cucumber.* **SENSITIVE SKIN:** *Seek out products that are hypoallergenic, meaning they're free of known irritating chemicals, perfumes, and dyes.* **NORMAL SKIN:** *Requires a delicate balance between scrubbing away dead skin cells and sealing in moisture. Decide whether the T-zone area—forehead, nose, chin—tends toward oiliness or dryness; there are products labeled both "normal to oily" and "normal to dry."*

Mineral. "Taking the water cure" is a centuries-old ritual. What reportedly made waters healing were minerals such as sulfur, calcium, magnesium, fluoride. None of those minerals can be absorbed into the skin, but try telling that to a believer. Mud, whether it comes from the Dead Sea or your backyard, is nothing more than clay or sand and water with traces of minerals. Slathered on the skin, it acts as an astringent, drawing out oil, bacteria, and dirt. The latest in mineral treatments is called thalassotherapy, where the bather is dipped in sea water and wrapped in mineral-rich seaweed. You don't need to buy commercial products—simply soak dried seaweed, such as kombu, and apply the slippery gel to your skin. The seaweed temporarily makes the skin smoother; some claim that the vitamins and minerals, applied topically, have anti-oxidant properties. Maybe. But do we pay for mud baths because of the health benefits or because they're the only socially sanctioned way to revel in slime?

Herbal. Herbs do some fairly miraculous things. Who was the first to discover that certain leaves, when rolled and smoked, allowed us to see God and bore people silly at parties? Or realized that rosemary was a pick-me-up, and that chamomile adds highlights to blond and brown hair? A seventeenth-century French courtesan came up with an herbal bath anti-wrinkle potion: Ninon de Lenclos bathed daily in a concoction of mint, lavender, thyme, rosemary, and leeks, keeping her skin smooth until old age. You can buy commercially prepared herbs, or you can skip the fancy packaging and head straight to a local herbalist.

MUSCLE RELIEF
Place a half cup of bay leaves in a pint of just-boiled water, and let them steep for twenty minutes. Remove leaves, pour the liquid into a warm bath. Sit in the tub for fifteen minutes.

MIND RELIEF
For a traditional herb-soak bath, take a teaspoonful each of rosemary, basil, dill, mint, thyme, sage, and chamomile, tie them up in a cheesecloth bag, and suspend the bag under the bathtub tap while the water is running.

Fruit. Maybe it was an attempt to keep him from straying. It didn't work, but Julius Caesar's wife is credited with inventing the first fruit bath. Her recipe: 20 pounds of crushed strawberries, 2 pounds of crushed raspberries. Those of us who'd rather not go through life dyed a delicate shade of pink have other alternatives: apricot, orange, or papaya. Fruits are valued for their astringent, refreshing qualities. Nuts are also popular in the bath: jojoba, almond, coconut— all are rich in oil, and effective as moisturizers. Almond extract will make you amorous or edible, or maybe both.

DOLLARS & SCENTS

Orange is believed to relieve stress: some Japanese offices waft orange scent through their air-conditioning ducts to minimize worker angst.

"Son of a bitch had to make it red. Lime would have gone much better with this room."

ALEXANDER WOOLCOTT,
—The New Yorker *drama critic upon finding that playwright Charles MacArthur had filled his bathtub with raspberry Jell-O.*

Vegetable. "There are many ways to love a vegetable," the unsurpassable food writer M.F.K. Fisher once wrote. "The most sensible way is to love it well treated." What she wasn't considering was how well vegetables can treat you. Consider the cucumber. For centuries women have been placing cucumber slices over their eyes to relieve puffiness. Vegetables may lack the fragrance benefits of fruits and flowers, but a few of them, such as cucumbers and carrots, are astringent and bracing to the skin. There's even a new exfoliating bath vegetable for the Nineties—blue corn, grown and sold by Pueblo Indians in the Southwest. Grains of the milled corn in soap or body lotions are gentle skin scrubbers.

STINK PROOF *The most popular vegetable bath of all time? Undoubtedly the tomato bath, used as an antidote to skunk spray. (All right, the tomato's a fruit, but let's not get picky.)* RECIPE: *Take one dog that's been spritzed. Dump two gallons of tomato juice over him (unless he's, say, a Chihuahua—then vary quantity accordingly). Massage dog all over. Run like hell when dog climbs out of the bathtub and shakes.*

Milk. Is it a symbolic return to the womb, to bathe ourselves in the fluid of our mothers? Or is there something even more covertly sexual about it? Milk baths have been popular since Nero's second wife, Poppaea, began traveling with a train of asses to provide milk for her daily ablutions. Proteins in the milk leave the skin feeling smooth and silky. For a bath that's both moisturizing and politically correct, look for The Body Shop's Powdered Milk Bath with avocado oil and oat flour: it's made from surplus milk that the European Commission was planning to throw away.

FAMOUS MILK BATHERS

Mary, Queen of Scots
Cleopatra (like Poppaea, in asses' milk)
Princess Pauline Borghese, the sister of Napoleon
Anna Held, the first great Ziegfeld star
Brooke Shields in Louis Malle's Pretty Baby

MILK BATH RECIPE

Steep favorite herbs in cold milk for several hours, strain, and add the herb-infused milk to your bath.

MILK TOAST RECIPE

1 slice toast, 3/4 inch thick, buttered, and salted. Place in bowl and pour over it 1 cup hot milk.

Floral. Myrna Loy lolled in a petal-strewn tub in the 1933 movie *The Barbarian*, and for a moment every woman in the audience wanted to run away with her Arabian potentate. With no potentate immediately available, we settle happily for the water and the flowers: bergamot, ylang-ylang, jasmine, camellia, carnation, and lavender. Rose is perhaps the most popular of florals. The scent is the most womanly, as the flower is man's analogue for Womanhood itself, combining both beauty and thorny danger. Odd, isn't it, that the idea of being "fresh as a daisy" has not translated into a soap or oil.

BATH DIVAS
Venus
Marie Antoinette
Lana Turner in The Ziegfeld Girl, *1941*
Paulette Goddard in Unconquered, *1947*
Marilyn Monroe, getting her toe stuck in bathtub faucet in The Seven Year Itch, *1955*

BATH DIVAS, CHAMPAGNE EDITION
Sarah Bernhardt, who claimed that champagne made her skin smooth

CHAMPAGNE ALERT
The idea of a champagne bath is much better than the reality: in fact, the alcohol and carbonation in champagne will burn delicate vaginal tissue.

47

B A S I C S

When you get back to basics, you're buying free-dom—freedom from the compulsion to own every bath bauble on the shelf. You want to accomplish three things in the bath: cleansing, exfoliating, and moistur-izing. The variable in the equation is fragrance: you may want to exude Chanel Cristalle, or then again you may prefer to smell like a banana. It's your choice.

"Slap-dash grooming may get by
with the mud-pie set, but it doesn't put any
diamonds on any ring fingers."

"THE WONDERFUL WORLD OF THE BATH,"

a 1964 brochure by The Cleanliness Bureau

Soaps. Think of soaps—"whether gel, powder or bar"—as a kind of inanimate Push Me–Pull You. One end of the soap molecule attracts water; the other end attracts oil and dirt, but repels water. With a kind of pushing and pulling action, the soap loosens the bonds holding dirt to the skin. But here's a dirty little secret: unless you live in a Third World country where infectious diseases are common, it doesn't really matter to your health whether you're clean or not. Skin is as indifferent to dirt as the average four-year-old.

MILESTONES IN SOAP HISTORY 1853: *William Gladstone, Chancellor of the Exchequer in England, protests the use of soap, calling it "injurious to the comfort and health of the people."* 1884: *Shopkeeper William Hesketh Lever decides to market individual bars of soap, instead of the huge "ingots" soap was normally available in. He stamped the bars with the name "Sunlight," and added citronella as a fragrance.* 1911: *First bath collection of soap introduced in France by Paul Poiret.* 1937: *The Guiding Light, America's first soap opera, began broadcasting on NBC radio; it moved to television in 1952, forever changing how housewives in America spend their time.*

SOAPSTONE

MAGNO

VEGETABLE SOAP WITH HONEY
AND LAVENDER

ANNICK GOUTAL
GARDENIA PASSION

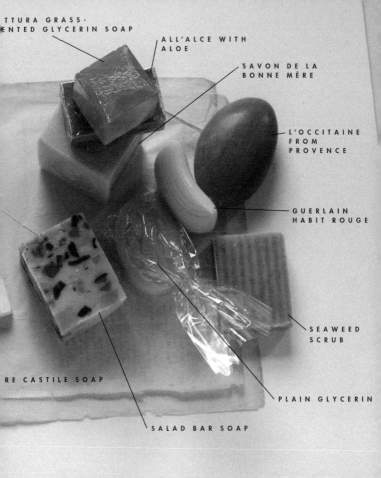

TTURA GRASS-
ENTED GLYCERIN SOAP

ALL'ALCE WITH
ALOE

SAVON DE LA
BONNE MÈRE

L'OCCITAINE
FROM
PROVENCE

GUERLAIN
HABIT ROUGE

SEAWEED
SCRUB

RE CASTILE SOAP

PLAIN GLYCERIN

SALAD BAR SOAP

Salts. Colored, fragrant bath salts always seem to suggest a mini–sea adventure, so closely do they resemble the pebbles we use on the floors of tropical fish tanks. In fact, salts are particularly helpful in relaxing tired muscles and joints. Epsom salts are chiefly medicinal: they relieve constipation by drawing water into the intestine. A good scrub with them can also be used to exfoliate skin. Scented sea salts, containing salt and seaweed extract, may contain a wide variety of trace minerals, including iodine; in addition to soothing itchy skin, they reportedly dilate the pores and relax the muscles, allowing the absorption of soluble vitamins into the skin. Incidentally, thanks to a new water extraction method, sea salts do not smell fishy.

WHAT'S AGE GOT TO DO WITH IT?
Percentage of women who use bubble baths, gels, and oils: 35%
Percentage who use bath salts and cubes: 23%
Bubble baths, gels, and oils are favored among 20–34-year-olds, while bath salts and cubes appeal to 55–64-year-olds.

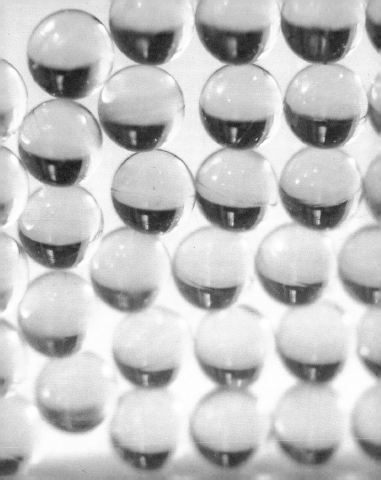

Oils. In Egypt, only the wealthiest could afford perfumed oils for the bath; the poor rubbed their bodies with palm oil. Whether you use beads or liquid, a dip in an oil bath is the ultimate in moisturizing. Oils may be scented or unscented; many contain vitamin E, reputed to be a skin soother. They may be poured into the bath, or, if they're in bath-bead form, "melted" under rushing hot water. (A parental caution: bath beads look good enough to eat and some kids do—keep them out of reach.) Remember that oils can stain clothes; so, if you like to wash your undies while bathing, don't do so when taking an oil bath. To avoid drying the skin, anyone who bathes every day should soak in oil at least twice a week. Some bath oils also double as soap; check the label.

"I'm a Pisces, so naturally I'm very much at home in water."

ELIZABETH TAYLOR,

who had her own bath triumph in Cleopatra, *1963*

Left to right:

CARBALINE BAGNO
Schiuma al timo

LE JARDIN RETROUVÉ
Sandalwood bain parfumé

MON JARDINET
Lavender bath oil

NEAL'S YARD REMEDIES
Exotic bath oil

LES HERBES
Eucalyptus natural gel

WILD WOOD FLOWER & HERB LTD
Comfrey leaf bath gel

CULPEPER STEPHANOTIS
Bath elixir

CULPEPER

TRADITIONAL VICTORIAN MUSTARD BATH

9 oz nett 255 g

Made in England
Culpeper Ltd 21 Bruton St
London England

Powder. Iconographically, bubble baths have conveyed both female wiles and female dependence. Think Busby Berkeley movies; think Julia Roberts in *Pretty Woman*. Of course, the bubble bath can translate into vulnerability; recall Michael Caine's doomed patients in *Dressed to Kill*. Lavish baths should carry a warning: bubbles that last too long signal the presence of environmentally unsound detergent. Look for "all natural" ingredients on the label. Most bath powders, including bubble baths, are variations of soap: pour the powder under running water and enjoy.

MUSTARD
BENEFITS
Mustard baths, in addition to the mild tingle they cause by bringing blood to the skin's surface, reportedly bring on a woman's period.

MUSTARD BATH
RECIPE
Dissolve 1 tablespoon of hot mustard powder in a cup of just-boiled water, and add it to your bathwater. Sit in the bath for twenty minutes, then rinse off under the shower.

HOW MUCH
Follow directions on package carefully; whether it's bath oil, beads, powder, or bubble bath, adding too much can irritate the skin.

T   O   O   L   S

What did man have before towels and bath mitts and sponges and loofahs? Leaves to scrub with, sun and wind to dry. Take an outdoor bath sometime, and learn how, occasionally, forgoing the man-made tools can be its own reward. However, a back scrubber is man's single greatest contribution to sensuality—at least, before batteries were invented.

"I believe I will dip my pink-
and-white body in yon Roman tub.
I feel a bit gritty after the affairs
of the day."

W . C . F I E L D S , My Little Chickadee, *1 9 4 0*

Scrubs and Towels. Maybe it's a bit creepy to know you're washing with a dead animal, but try to take it in stride: natural sponges are the fossilized skeletons of complex marine organisms. Until the eighteenth century, they were thought to be solidified sea foam. Loofahs are dried plants, a member of the cucumber family. Whether it's a loofah, a sponge, or any one of dozens of bath mitts made from everything from Irish linen to goat hair, the idea here is to exfoliate dead skin cells. When choosing a bath towel, look for three characteristics: texture, size (as in other areas of life, size really does count), and absorbency. Egyptian cotton has extra-long fibers that make the towels wonderfully smooth yet durable. Pima is an American-grown cotton that is less expensive and just as absorbent, but a bit less durable. China may have invented silk, but Americans can take pride in their own homegrown ultra-absorbent bath fabric: terry cloth. The first terry was created in 1900 by Canon.

MOTTURA
AGAVE CLOTH

SEA SPONGE

IL MASSAGGIO
RASSODANTE
SISAL BACK SCRUB

NAIL BRUSH

TERRY CLOTH
WASH MITT

SCRUB
BRUSH

IL MASSAGGIO
RASSODANTE
SISAL BATH MITT

SOFT SCRUB
BRUSH

SISTINA
BATH BRUSH

Pumice. Real pumice is a stone related to granite, but porous and light enough to float; it's made of volcanic lava that's solidified and permeated with gas bubbles. Everyone can remember growing up with a piece of pumice lying around the bathtub, to rub off calluses on the hands and feet. Now pumice has gone high-tech. Some may be made out of terra-cotta or other natural materials; others have soap embedded in the pores, for a lather-and-scrub effect. The grain of the pumice determines its use: smaller-grained stone *(far left)* for allover body use, and a larger-grained stone *(near left)* for rough areas, such as hands and feet. Pumice is also a must when you're at the beach—the grit from the rock removes sand from arms and legs. Use caution with pumice and other exfoliators: while they can lift dirt, germs, makeup, and even environmental pollutants away from the skin's surface, they can also remove the skin's natural oils. If you love to scrub, use superfatted soap and a good moisturizer.

Kid Stuff. Most kids feel about dirt the way Henry VIII felt about wives: the more, the better. But several companies have gotten savvy about what parents want in their kids' baths: naturally, non-eye-stinging, gentle, environmentally conscious products, including everything from baby oils, shampoos, and cleansing bars to The Body Shop's bath soaps in the shape of endangered species. A word of warning: babies can drown in as little as an inch of water, so don't turn your back on the little ones.

HOW TO TAKE A BATH LIKE A CHILD

1. *As a scientific experiment, scrunch up at one end of the tub and slosh back and forth really, really fast, to determine how much water you can displace out of the tub and onto the bathroom floor.* 2. *Make a Princess Di crown out of soap bubbles.* 3. *Cast a magic spell over your washcloth, and watch it become a dolphin that can turn cartwheels in the water.* 4. *Drag every toy you own into the tub with you; when your parents tell you some of them don't belong there and may in fact electrocute you, whimper piteously for one hour.* 5. *Yell "Help! I'm drowning,"* *and watch how quickly your parents can move, even though they're old.*

soap dish

Travel. When on a business trip, remember that the sample-size bath products found in expensive hotels are meant to be stolen and used later in less expensive hotels, when you're paying out of your own pocket. The ideal travel kit is compact, durable, compartmentalized, and lined with plastic. Never travel with breakable glass bottles or metal that will set off airplane metal detectors. Also resist the temptation to turn on that mysterious overhead tanning lamp in the bathrooms of mid-priced hotels everywhere. God only knows what that thing does to your skin.

BEST BATHTUBS
The best bathtubs are found in England, where 60% of all people take baths as compared with 20% in the U.S.

BEST TEMPERATURE
In Switzerland, the hot water is hottest and the cold water is coldest.

DOWN UNDER
It's true: in Australia and New Zealand, the water goes down the drain counterclockwise.

TRAVEL SOAK RECIPE
For portable relief, go to a health food store and buy a bottle of rosa gallica. Put a few drops in the bath at day's end, drape a washcloth over your eyes, and breathe deeply.

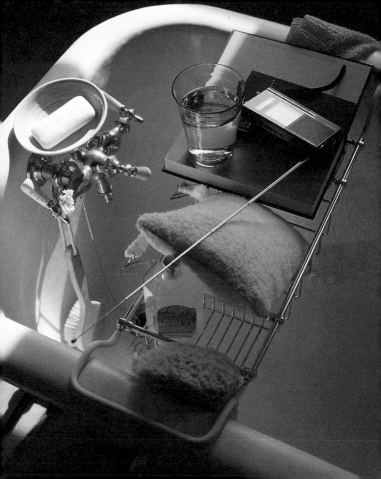

Bath Tray. A bath tray is a defiant little bath treat, an accessory that says, "I'm going to spend the afternoon lying here. Just try to stop me." Whether it's wood, brass, or plastic, the ideal bath tray includes a compartment for sponges, razors, or soap, a place for balancing a glass of wine, and, most important, a book rest to keep your book balanced at an appropriate angle and away from the suds.

A BATH IS NOT JUST FOR BATHING *You can also: do dictation, eat, sketch, read this book, talk on the phone, do the crossword puzzle, fall in love, do the dishes, write letters, sing, play with boats, test tidal theories, listen to Leonard Cohen, make major decisions, work cat's cradles, catch up on magazines, watch TV, gaze at the stars (if you have a skylight or are outdoors), send faxes, practice an instrument, or, best of all, be alone.* BATH FACTS *Percentage of people who read in the bathroom: 40%/ who smoke: 20%/ who listen to radio: 14%/ who talk on the phone: 8%* SHOWERS VS. BATHS *Average number of baths a week by women who prefer baths: 4.5/ Average number of showers: 7.5/ Average number of baths a week by men who prefer baths: 3.2/ Average number of showers: 8*

Containers. Raymond Chandler called the cosmetics industry "that confidence racket"; but we all love a good con game. Half the reason we love a beauty product is not for what it does, but for the way it looks. Until very recently, cosmetics companies have had some of the most wasteful packaging: think about the amount of paper and plastic that surrounds one little tube of lipstick. The move in recent years has been toward environmentally sound packaging that's still a sensual delight. Look for packaging that doesn't contain layers of cardboard and cellophane. Also, look for recycled or recyclable materials, such as cloth, glass, and some plastics.

FILL 'EM UP *The Body Shop has pioneered the recyclable container. These days, you can get a price break if you bring an old Body Shop container back to the store for a refill. You can also do a bit of conserving on your own; many companies are selling economy-size versions of their products. You can transfer portions of these gels, powders, etc., into beautiful antique bottles or jars that will make any common cosmetics shelf into a toilette.*

first aid. Whether you're

making a mineral bath or avoiding a heart attack or washing your face,

here's everything you need to know to make the bath sensual and safe.

SKIN

THE TRUTH ABOUT SKIN AND MOISTURIZERS

Skin aging is not, as many think, caused by a loss of moisture. A seventy-five-year-old woman has as much water in her cells as a twenty-year-old. Rather, it's caused by the cells losing their capacity to regenerate, slowing down their production of the elastin and collagen fibers that give the skin its softness and elasticity.

MOISTURIZING

Moisturizers do not have any clinical effect on underlying skin. What they do is temporarily seal in moisture, making your skin smoother-looking. Always moisturize while your skin is still damp—right out of the bath. People who spend a lot of time out in the sun should look for moisturizers with sunscreen.

TO EASE SUNBURN

Mix kelp with baking soda and salt, and add the mixture to your bath.

FOR ACNE

If you're prone to acne, don't scrub or use washcloths. Follow cleansing with a toner containing the drying agent salicylic acid.

WASHCLOTH VS. SPONGE

Whether you use a washcloth or sponge for soaping and rinsing is a matter of personal preference, although washcloths tend more quickly than sponges to become slimy when wet, and hard and abrasive when dry, due to soap deposits.

CAVEAT EMPTOR

"RECYCLED"?

So far, there are no laws governing the use of such words as "recyclable" or "recycled." The entire package may be recycled, or only a small part of it. If it's important to you, call the manufacturer to find out.

"NATURAL"?

Similarly, the term "all-natural" is used with abandon. Almost no products are entirely all natural, although some rely more on natural ingredients than others. However, just because an ingredient is made in a lab doesn't mean it's bad for you.

SEA PLANT PRODUCTS?

Examine the list of ingredients on the package. Since this list is required by law to be given in order from greatest to least, sea plants should be listed toward the beginning to be present in sufficient quantity to be effective. Furthermore, use of the CTFA term "seaweed extract" ensures that active sea plant substances have been retained; those labeled "kelp" or "algin" may be sea products in powdered or chemically processed forms.

GLOBAL WARNING

Be careful when taking a bath in Mexico. On the spigots, "H" = "helado" (= cold); C = "caliente" (= hot).

SOAPS AND SCRUBS

ALOE

Aloe is a plant in the cactus family known for its skin-healing medicinal properties. The gel squeezed from the aloe leaf, applied directly to a burn, soothes and heals. In soap, it's an excellent moisturizer.

ANTI-BACTERIAL

Soaps may wash bacteria from the skin's surface, but only a soap labeled "anti-bacterial" actually kills bacteria. A word of warning: overuse of anti-bacterial soap may be irritating to the skin.

CASTILE

Castile soap is derived from olive oil from the Castile region of Spain.

DEODORANT SOAPS

Use deodorant soaps only for sweat-prone spots; on other parts of the body, they may be too drying.

FRAGRANCE SOAP

Most soaps have a fragrance, but some are valued primarily for their exotic scent—for example, Annick Goutal's "Gardenia Passion."

GLYCERIN

Glycerin is an effective moisturizer, but see-through glycerin soap does an astounding vanishing act; buy bars in quantity.

MOISTURIZING SOAP

Moisturizing soap is usually "superfatted," created specifically to reduce dryness and seal moisture into the skin.

SALAD SOAP

Salad soap is recycled from bits and pieces of many kinds of soap.

SCRUB
A scrub is any soap infused with tiny-granule exfoliants for sloughing off dead skin while cleansing.

SOAPSTONE
Soapstone is a porous mineral made mostly of talc. It has a soapy feel, and acts chiefly as an exfoliant.

SMELL

FRAGRANCE TIMETABLE
The form of the scent you use determines how long it will last on your skin:
Perfume: 5–6 hours
Cologne: 2–3 hours
Toilet water: 2–3 hours
Perfume in lotion: 3–4 hours
Bath oil: 5–6 hours
Bath powder: 2–3 hours

AROMATHERAPY

INVIGORATING SCENTS
Clove, rosemary, spruce, juniper, lemon, peppermint

STRESS RELIEVERS
Vanilla, tuberose, nutmeg, spruce, juniper, orange

RELAXING SCENTS
Jasmine, chamomile, geranium, marjoram, lavender, rose

APHRODISIACS
Sandalwood, ylang-ylang, sage

FRAGRANCE AND CULTURE
There's a pharmacopoeia of herbs recommended for every conceivable mood. But remember— our associations with odor vary from person to person, and even from culture to culture. Take suki: most Japanese love the scent, which smells like the inside of a traditional wood bath. To them, it's very relaxing; to Americans, it smells like Pine-Sol.

HOW-TOS

SELF-MASSAGE IN THE BATH
Breathing deeply and rhythmically, press your fingertips into your scalp and move slowly with clockwise circles from your forehead toward the back of your neck. Then, with your hands still cupped around the back of your head, place your thumbs at the base of your skull and methodically move them from the center toward each ear, making little circles. Run your fingers up and down the back of your ears a few times. Press your fingertips into your cheeks and make deep circular motions. Better yet, have someone else do this for you.

BEGONE, BATHTUB RINGS

Why do rings form in some bathtubs and not in others? It doesn't really depend on how dirty you are—it's the hardness of the water that counts. In hard water, the soap reacts with the salts that make the water hard, forming grimy-looking "rings." The best way to get rid of a ring: old-fashioned elbow grease, with a gentle abrasive made for today's tubs. Don't use scouring powder, unless you have an old-fashioned iron enamel tub.

HOW TO WASH YOUR FACE

Lather soap in the palms of your hands. Massage lather into damp skin in circular motion to loosen dead cells and dissolve grease. Rinse with several splashes of lukewarm water to remove all traces of soap and excess oils. Pat—don't rub dry. Try not to get too obsessed with the whole process. If you screw it up, your face will not fall off.

RECIPES

HERBAL BATH

(from Total Health *magazine, Dec. 1992)*
1 ounce pennyroyal herb
2 ounces rosemary leaves
2 ounces rosebuds
4 ounces lavender flowers
2 ounces marjoram herb
1 ounce patchouli herb
10 drops orris root oil
10 drops sandalwood oil
5 drops bergamot oil

Pre-blend oils; put all flowers in blender or small food mill. Then combine oils and flowers. Use a tablespoonful or two per bath.

MINERAL BATH

(Recipe makes 2 1/2 cups, and you only need a few tablespoons in bath.)
4 ounces clay or starch
8 ounces baking soda
60 drops lavender oil
30 drops patchouli oil
30 drops muguet oil
Pre-blend the oils, blend all ingredients, then mix and sieve.

FLORAL BATH

1 cup chamomile
1/2 cup rose petals
1 cup lavender
1 cup lemon verbena
Use only 1/2 cup of mixture per bath; wrap in muslin bag, and place under running water.

MORNING-AFTER BATH

(for hangovers)
Put 5–10 drops of clove oil into bathwater. While in the bath, quarter a lemon and rub the juicy side under each armpit. To get rid of a headache, follow up by eating ten strawberries; for an upset stomach, drink a cup of ginger tea (four pieces of ginger steeped for ten minutes in just-boiled water).

where. A Chic Simple store looks

out on the world beyond its shop window. Items are practical and

comfortable and will work with pieces bought elsewhere. The

store can be a cottage industry or a global chain, but even with an

international vision it is still rooted in tradition, quality, and value.

United States

CALIFORNIA

FILLAMENTO
2185 Fillmore Street
San Francisco, CA 94115
415/931-2224
(Bath soaps and salts)

FRED SEGAL
ENVIRONMENT
420 Broadway
Santa Monica, CA 90401
310/394-7088
(Bath and body products)

MOTHER'S MARKET
225 East 17th Street
Costa Mesa, CA 92627
714/631-4741
(Bath salts, bubble bath)

PALMETTO
1034 Montana Avenue
Santa Monica, CA 90403
310/395-6687
(Bath salts, bath oils)

FLORIDA

BEACH NEWS
651 Washington Avenue
Miami Beach, FL 33139
305/672-0081
(Bath soaps, oils, shower gels)

FAST BUCK FREDDIE'S
500 Duval Street
Key West, FL 33040
305/294-2007
(Bath soaps, body lotions, talcs)

GEORGIA

RICH'S
Lenox Square Shopping Mall
3393 Peachtree Road
Atlanta, GA 30326
404/231-2611
(Fine bath products)

LOUISIANA

ESTELLA'S
200 Broadway, Suite #101
New Orleans, LA 70118
504/865-9000
*(Bath and body products,
linens)*

NEW MEXICO

WILD OATS
1090 South St. Francis Drive
Santa Fe, NM 87501
505/983-5333
(Seaweed, herbal baths, salts)

NEW YORK

ABC CARPET & HOME
888 Broadway
New York, NY 10003
212/473-3000
(Soaps, towels, accessories)

AD HOC SOFTWARES
410 West Broadway
New York, NY 10012
212/925-2652
*(Soaps, lotions, towels,
accessories)*

AKASHIMAYA
693 Fifth Avenue
New York, NY 10022
212/350-0100
(Skincare and bath products)

AVEDA
409 Madison Avenue
New York, NY 10022
212/832-2416
*(Moisturizers, bubble bath,
liquid soaps)*

BATH ISLAND
469 Amsterdam Avenue
New York, NY 10024
212/787-9415
(Bubble bath, soaps, loofahs)

BERGDORF GOODMAN
754 Fifth Avenue
New York, NY 10019
212/753-7300
*(Bath products and
accessories)*

DEAN & DELUCA
560 Broadway
New York, NY 10012
212/431-1691
(Soaps, body oils)

FELISSIMO
10 West 56th Street
New York, NY 10022
212/956-4438
(Bath soaps, gels, lotions)

KIEHL'S
109 Third Avenue
New York, NY 10003
212/475-3400
(Bath and skin products)

PORTICO BED & BATH
379 West Broadway
New York, NY 10012
212/941-7800
(Towels, soaps, oils, scrubs)

TERRA VERDE
TRADING CO.
120 Wooster Street
New York, NY 10012
212/925-4533
*(Environmentally correct
soaps, towels, and accessories)*

WOLFMAN-GOLD &
GOOD
116 Greene Street
New York, NY 10012
212/431-1888
*(Soaps, towels, and
accessories)*

VERMONT

POLO/RALPH LAUREN
FACTORY STORE
Routes 11 and 30
Manchester, VT 05255
802/362-2340
(Bath towels)

SEVENTH GENERATION
176 Battery Street
Burlington, VT 05401
802/658-7770
802-655-6777 for catalogue
(Soaps, towels, bathmats)

BARNEYS NEW YORK
106 Seventh Avenue
New York, NY 10011
212/929-9000
800/777-0087 for U.S.
listings
(Soaps, oils, lotions, sponges)

BATH & BODY WORKS
89 South Street
Pier 17
New York, NY 10038
212/693-0247
(Bath oils, soaps, body lotions)

BED BATH & BEYOND
620 Avenue of the Americas
New York, NY 10012
212/255-3550
516/424-1070 for U.S.
listings
(Oils, soaps, bathrobes, towels)

HENRI BENDEL
712 Fifth Avenue
New York, NY 10019
212/247-1100
(Bath soaps, lotions, oils)

BLOOMINGDALE'S
1000 Third Avenue
New York, NY 10022
212/355-5900 for U.S.
listings
(Bath products and accessories)

THE BODY SHOP
45 Horsehill Road
Cedar Knolls, NJ 07927
201/984-9200 for U.S.
listings
71/436-5681 for U.K.
listings
(Bath and body products)

CASWELL-MASSEY
518 Lexington Avenue
New York, NY 10017
212/755-2254
*(Natural sponges, bath
brushes, herbal baths, soaps)*

CONRAN'S HABITAT
160 East 54th Street
New York, NY 10022
212/371-2225
(Bath soaps, towels, accessories)

CRABTREE & EVELYN
1310 Madison Avenue
New York, NY 10128
212/289-3923
(Soaps, body creams, talc)

CRATE & BARREL
646 North Michigan Avenue
Chicago, IL 60611
312/787-5900
(Bathroom accessories)

DAYTON HUDSON'S,
MARSHALL FIELD'S,
TARGET
700 On The Mall
Minneapolis, MN 55402
612/375-2200
(Bath products and accessories)

DILLARD'S PARK
PLAZA
Markham & University
Little Rock, AR 72205
501/661-0053
(Bath products and accessories)

EMPORIO ARMANI
110 Fifth Avenue
New York, NY 10011
212/727-3240
212/570-1122 for
international listings
*(Soaps, crystals, salts,
bathrobes)*
Catalogue available

GARDEN BOTANIKA
Washington Square Mall
9508 S.W. Washington
Square Boulevard
Tigard, OR 97233
503/620-1975
800/877-9603 for West
Coast listings
(Body scrubs and lotions)

GOODEBODIES
330 Columbus Avenue
New York, NY 10023
212/721-9317
(Loofahs, bath oils, gels)
Catalogue available

H₂0
65 Madison Avenue
New York, NY 10022
212/767-5986
800/242-BATH for listings
in the U.S. and Canada
(Bath, beauty, aromatherapy)

HOLD EVERYTHING
P.O. Box 7807
San Francisco, CA 94120
800/421-2264 for catalogue
and store listings
(Bathroom accessories)

HOME DEPOT
449 Roberts Court Road
Kennesaw, GA 30144
404/433-8211
(Bathroom accessories)

R.H. MACY & CO. INC.
(BULLOCK'S, I. MAGNIN,
AÉROPOSTALE)
MACY'S HERALD
SQUARE
151 West 34th Street
New York, NY 10001
212/695-4400 for East Coast
listings

MACY'S WEST
170 O'Farrell Street
San Francisco, CA 94102
415/393-3457 for West
Coast listings
(Bath products and accessories)

NEIMAN MARCUS
1618 Main Street
Dallas, TX 75201
214/741-6911
(Bath products and accessories)

NORDSTROM
1501 Fifth Avenue
Seattle, WA 98191
206/628-2111
800/285-5800 for catalogue
(Bath products and accessories)

ORIGINS
402 West Broadway
New York, NY 10013
212/572-4100
800/723-7310 for U.S.
listings
(Skin care, sensory therapy oils)

PARISIAN
2100 River Chase Galleria
Birmingham, AL 35244
205/987-4200
205/940-4000 for U.S.
listings
(Bath products and accessories)

PIER 1 IMPORTS
P.O. Box 961020
Ft. Worth, TX 76161
800/447-4371 for U.S.
listings
(Bath beads, crystals, soaps)

POLO/RALPH LAUREN
HOME COLLECTION
867 Madison Avenue
New York, NY 10021
212/606-2100
212/318-7000 for U.S.
listings
(Bath soaps and towels)

SAKS FIFTH AVENUE
611 Fifth Avenue
New York, NY 10022
212/753-4000 for U.S.
listings
*(Bath products and
accessories)*

URBAN OUTFITTERS
1801 Walnut Street
Philadelphia, PA 19103
215/569-3131
215/564-2313 for U.S.
listings
(Bath soaps, oils, lotions)

CATALOGUES AND MAIL ORDER

AGRARIA
1148 Taylor Street
San Francisco, CA 94108
800/824-3632
(Soaps, bath essence)

AVON
800/FOR-AVON
(Personal bath products)

CHAMBERS
P.O. Box 7841
San Francisco, CA 94120
800/334-9790
(Soaps, towels, bath crystals)

EARTHEN JOYS
1412 Eleventh Street
Astoria, OR 97103
503/325-0426
(Bath products)

ECCO BELLA
125 Pompton Plains
Crossroad
Wayne, NJ 07470
800/322-9344
(Cruelty-free moisturizing cream, facial cleansers, skin toners)

REAL GOODS TRADING CORPORATION
966 Mazzoni Street
Ukiah, CA 95482
800/762-7325
(Bath soaps)

WALNUT ACRES
Walnut Acres Road
Penns Creek, PA 17862
717/837-0601
(Organic soaps, moisturizing creams)

INTERNATIONAL LISTINGS

Australia

MELBOURNE

GEORGES AUSTRALIA LTD.
162 Collins Street
3/283-5555
(Personal bath products)

SYDNEY

HARBOURSIDE
Darling Harbour
2/552-0261 for store information
(Boutiques selling bath products)

GRACE BROS.
436 George Street
2/218-1111
(Bath oils and lotions)

REMO MAIL-ORDER CATALOGUE
Oxford at Crown Street
8/029-714
(Bath products by mail)

Canada

MONTREAL

OGILVY
1307 St. Catherine Street West
514/842-7711
(Perfumed soaps and lotions)

QUEBEC

PUR ET SIMPLE
Ayers Cliff
Quebec City, Quebec
418/522-3645
(Soaps, lotions, herbal baths)

France

PARIS

A L'EPI D'OR
17, rue des Bernardins
75005
46/33-08-47
(Antique bath furniture and accessories)

AUX SALLES DE BAINS
RETRO
29-31, rue des Dames
75017
43/87-88-00
(Retro bathroom design)

BEAUTÉ DIVINE
40, rue Saint-Sulpice
75006
43/26-25-31
(Bathroom accessories)

CASA BLU
27, rue du Cherche-Midi
75006
45/48-83-35
(Robes and bath towels)

LA BOUTIQUE DE
MARIE-CLAIRE
2, rue Berger
75008
42/33-74-53
(Bathroom accessories)

GALERIES LAFAYETTE
40, boulevard Haussmann
75009
42/82-34-56
(Bath products and accessories)

L'AROMARINE
45, rue Saint-Louis-en-L'île
46/34-26-32
(Personal bath products)

LE SAPONIFÈRE
59, rue Bonaparte
75006
42/97-42-14
(Flower-based soaps)

UN AIR DE PROVENCE
48, rue Saint-Antoine
42/78-82-56
(Natural soaps, loofahs)

YVES ROCHER
238, rue de Rivoli
75001
42/97-53-29
(Natural bath oils, scrubs)

PROVENCE

SANTOLINE
34, boulevard Victor Hugo
St. Rémy-de-Provence
13210
90/92-11-96
*(Oils, perfumes, and soaps
made in Provence)*

Germany

BERLIN

SELBACH
Kürfürstendamm 195/196
30/883-2526
(Personal bath products)

HAMBURG

MEY & EDLICH
Theatinerstrasse 7
89/290-0590
30/7915030 in Berlin
(Personal bath products)

Great Britain

LONDON

BRITISH HOME
STORES
71/262-3288
(Bathroom accessories)

THE CONRAN SHOP
LTD.
Michelin House
81 Fulham Road
SW3 6RD
71/589-7401
(Bath accessories)

COSMETICS TO GO
Freepost, Poole, Dorset,
BH15 1BR
800/373-366
(Personal bath products)

CRABTREE & EVELYN
LTD.
55-57 South Edwardes
Square
W8 6HP
71/603-1611
(Soaps, body creams, talc)

CZECH AND SPEAKE
LTD.
244-254 Cambridge Heath
Road
E2 9DA
81/980-4567
(Bath products and fittings)

GENERAL TRADING
COMPANY
144 Sloane Street
SW1X 9BL
71/730-0411
(Bathroom accessories)

HABITAT
Heals Building
196 Tottenham Court Road
W1P 9LD
71/255-2545
(Bathroom accessories)

HACKETTS
136-138 Sloane Street
SW1X 9AY
71/730-3331
(Toiletries)

HARRODS
87-135 Brompton Road
SW1X 7XL
071/730-1234
(Personal bath products)

HARVEY NICHOLLS
109-125 Knightsbridge,
SW1X 7RJ
71/235-5000
(Upscale department store)

HEALS
196 Tottenham Court Road
W1A 1BJ
71/636-1666
*(Stylish bathrooms and
accessories)*

HOUSE OF FRASER
LTD.
71/834-1515 for U.K. listings
(Bath products and accessories)

IDEAL-STANDARD LTD
P.O. Box 60
National Avenue
Kingston Upon Hull
North Humberside
HU5 4JE
71/482-46461
(Bath products)

JOHN LEWIS
Oxford Street
W1A 1EX
71/629-7711
(Bath products)

LIBERTY
210-220 Regent Street
W1R 6AH
71/734-1234
*(Bath products, towels,
accessories)*

MALLBONE OF
DEVIZES
93 Wimpole Street
W1
71/493-6298
(Very stylish bathrooms)

MARKS & SPENCER
PLC.
99 Kensington High Street
W8 5SQ
71/938-3711
(Bathrobes)

MUJI
26 Great Marlborough
Street
W1V 1HB
71/494-1197
*(No name brand bath
products)*

NEAL'S YARD
REMEDIES
1A Rossiter Road
Balham
SW12 9RY
81/675-7144
(Operates mail order service)

SELFRIDGES
400 Oxford Street
W1A 1AB
71/629-1234
(Bath products, furnishings)

TWYFORDS
BATHROOMS/DALTON
BATHROOM PRODUCTS
Lawton Road
Alsager, Stoke-on-Trent
ST7 2DF
270/879-777
(Bathroom accessories)

LITTLEHAMPTON

THE BODY SHOP
INTERNATIONAL PLC
Watersmead,
Littlehampton,
West Sussex, BN17 6LS
903-731500
(Personal bath products)

Italy

MILAN

FRETTE
via Manzoni, 11
2/86-43-39
(Terry cloth bathrobes and
towels)

ROME

IL BIANCO DI ELLEPI
via della Croce, 4
6/67-96-835
(Terry cloth towels and
bathrobes)

VENICE

JESURUM
Ponte Canonica, 4310
41/5206-177
(Linens for the bath)

Japan

TOKYO

ISETAN
3-14-1 Shinjuku-ku
Shinjuku-ku 160
3/3352-1111
(Personal bath products)

MITSUKOSHI
1-4-1 Nihonbashi
Muromachi
Chuo-ku
3/3241-3311
(Skincare and bath products)

MUJIRUSHI
5-50-6 Jingumae
Shibuya-ku
3/3407-4666
(No name brand bath products)

PARCO
14 Udagawa-cho
Shibuya-ku
3/3464-5111
(Skincare and bath products)

TAKASHIMAYA
2-4-1 Nihombashi
Chuo-ku
3/3211-4111
(Skincare and bath products)

TINAMARRY
20-13 Sarugakucho
Shibuya-ku
3/5489-9800
(Skincare and bath products)

TOKYU HANDS
12-18 Udagawa-cho
Shibuya-ku
3/5489-5111
(Bathroom accessories)

BATHS AND SPAS

BEVERLY HOT SPRINGS
308 North Oxford Avenue
Los Angeles, CA 90004
213/734-7000
(Bath/spa/massage)

CAP JULUCA
P.O. Box 240
Anguila, British West Indies
809/497-6666
800/323-0139
(Double tubs in hotel rooms)

CHICO HOT SPRINGS
LODGE
Drawer D
Pray, MT 59065
406/333-4933
(Mineral hot springs)

CRYSTAL SPA
Broadway
Saratoga Springs, NY 12866
518/584-2556
(Spa)

ESALEN INSTITUTE
Big Sur, CA 93920
408/667-3000
(Natural hot springs)

GREENBRIAR HOTEL
West Main Street
White Sulphur Springs, WV
24986
304/536-1110
(Natural sulfur springs; mineral baths)

HAIKKO MANOR SPA
06400 Porvoo, Finland
358/15-57601
358/15-1220399 (fax)
(Spa and baths)

HOT SPRINGS
National Park Service
Hot Springs, AR 71901
501/623-1433 for
information about six local
spas

HOTEL AQUINCUM
Arpod Fejedlem, 94
Budapest, Hungary 1036
361/188-6360
(Baths)

HOTEL GELLERT
Gellert Ter 1
Budapest, Hungary
361/16-64-92-82
(Art Deco hotel with famous baths)

LAPINNIEMI SPA
Lapinniemenranta 12
33180 Tampere, Finland
358/31-452081
358/31-597400 (fax)
(Spa and baths)

PORCHESTER SPA
Queensway
London W2
71/792-3980
(Public baths)

RUSSIAN BATHS
268 East Tenth Street
New York, NY 10009
212/674-9250
(Russian/Turkish baths/dry sauna, massage)

SAFETY HARBOUR SPA
105 North Bayshore Drive
Safety Harbour, FL 34695
813/726-1161
(Mineral springs pumped into hydrotherapy tubs, pool, Jacuzzi)

THE SPA HOTEL AND
MINERAL SPRINGS
100 North Indian Canyon
Drive
Palm Springs, CA 92262
619/325-1461
(Mineral baths)

TEN THOUSAND WAVES
Hyde Park Road
Santa Fe, NM 87504
505/982-9304
(Japanese health spa/private and public tubs/watsu massage)

THERMAL HOTEL
MARGITSZIGET
Margitsziget Island
Budapest, Hungary 1138
361/132-1100
(Baths)

RESOURCES

59 **BATH OILS** (from left) - Le Jardin
Retrouvé Sandalwood bain parfumé,
Barneys New York; Bergamot Rose
Lavender, Mon Jardinet Body & Bath Oil;
Neal's Yard Remedies Exotic Bath Oil,
Barneys New York; Eucalyptus Bath, Body &
Shampoo Gel, Les Herbes, Ltd.; Comfrey
Leaf Herbal Shower & Bath Gel, Wild
Wood Flower & Herb Ltd.; Culpeper
Stephanotis Bath Elixir, Barneys New York

60 **POWDER** - Culpeper Victorian Mustard
Bath, Barneys New York

64 **SILK WASH MITT** - Turquerie, Ad Hoc

66–67 **SCRUBS** (from left) - Sea sponge, Portico
Bed & Bath; Il Massaggio Rassodante sisal
back scrub, Barneys New York; Face
Scrub, Ad Hoc; Mottura Agave Cloth, Ad
Hoc; Soft Scrub Brush, Ad Hoc; Sistina
Bath Brush, Barneys, New York; Koh-i-
noor Nail Brush, Ad Hoc; Terry cloth
wash mitt, Ad Hoc; Sisal Bath Mitt, Il
Massaggio Rassodante; Scrub Brush,
Barneys New York

68 **OIL STONES** (from left) - All Body Use
Spa Stone, Ad Hoc; Hand & Foot Stone,
Ad Hoc

70 **BATH TOYS** - Penny Whistle, New York

72 **SOAP DISHES** (from left) - porcelain
soap dish, Howard Kaplan Bath Shop,
New York; ceramic soap dish, Vito Giallo
Antiques, New York; wooden and metal
soap dish, Dean & Deluca

73 **SOAP DISH** - Photographer's private
collection

74 **PLASTIC TRAVEL CONTAINERS** -
Woolworth's

76 **BATHTUB** - Urban Archaeology, New
York; **PORCELAIN & BRASS BATH
TRAY** - Howard Kaplan Bath Shop, New
York; **TERRY BATH PILLOW** - Memoire,
Malibu, Ca.; **BATH OIL** - Le Jardin
Retrouvé Sandalwood bain parfumé,
Barneys New York

78 **SOAPS** (from left) - La Compagnie de
Provence, Barneys New York; Natural
Acca Kappa Massage Soap, Portico Bed &
Bath; Valobra al burro di Cacao, Barneys
New York; Fleurs Des Alpes, Guerlain;
ANTIQUE GLASS JARS (far left and far
right) - Vito Giallo Antiques, New York;
GOLDEN OIL - Graminaceous Foam Bath
Softener by La Baignoire, Ad Hoc;
MUD BATH - Terme di Montecatini
Active Mud for Face & Body; **BOXED OIL** -
Carbaline Bagno Schiuma al Timo for
Emporio Armani

QUOTES

2 **JEFF MOSS**, "Rubber Duckie" (Festival
Attractions, 1970)

11 **GEORGE ELIOT**, *The Mill on the Floss*

12 **ERNIE PYLE**, *Bartlett's Famous Quotations*
(1955 edition)

27 **2 SAMUEL 11:2**

31 **MARK TWAIN**, *The Complete Essays of Mark
Twain* (Doubleday, 1985)

LIN YUTANG, *The Public Speaker's Treasure Chest* (Harper & Row, 1986)
ALEXANDER WOOLCOTT, *The Oxford Book of American Literary Anecdotes* (1981 edition)
THE CLEANLINESS BUREAU, *The Wonderful World of the Bath* (1964)
ELIZABETH TAYLOR, *Cleopatra*, 1963
W. C. FIELDS, *My Little Chickadee*, 1940
PETER MATTHIESSEN, *The Snow Leopard*

ACKNOWLEDGMENTS

Diane Ackerman, Ad Hoc Software, Barneys New York, Larry Becker, Rosie Boycott, Holly Brubach, Beth Chang, Tony Chirico, Ellen Cohen at Aveda, M. Scott Cookson, Copra Soap, Dean & Deluca, Lauri Del Commune, Dina Dell'Arciprete, Chris Di Maggio, Michael Drazen, Martyn Evans at The Body Shop, Marion Fouretier, Jane Friedman, Janice Goldklang, Annette Green at The Fragrance Foundation, Joanne Harrison, Patrick Higgins, Katherine Hourigan, Andy Hughes, Carol Janeway, Toru Kagami, George Lang, George Lange, Nicholas Latimer, Karen Leh, William Loverd, Joel Makower, Anne McCormick, Mary McEvoy, Sonny Mehta, Misako Noda, Portico Bed & Bath, Dorothy Schefer at Mirabella, Hellyn Sher, John Snowden, Anne-Lise Spitzer, Meg Stebbins, Robin Swados, Kim Turner, Shelley Wanger, Wayne Wolf, Alice Wong, Zona

A NOTE ON THE TYPE

The text of this book was set in New Baskerville, the ITC version of the typeface called Baskerville, which itself is a facsimile reproduction of types cast from molds made by John Baskerville (1706–1775) from his designs. Baskerville's original face was one of the forerunners of the type style known to printers as the "modern face"— a "modern" of the period A.D. 1800.

SEPARATION AND FILM PREPARATION BY
APPLIED GRAPHICS TECHNOLOGIES
Carlstadt, New Jersey

PRINTED AND BOUND BY
BERTELSMANN PRINTING & MANUFACTURING CORP.
Berryville, Virginia

"Simplicity is the whole secret of well-being."

PETER MATTHIESSEN *The Snow Leopard*